PATTERNS FOR IMPROVISATION
From The Beginning
By Frank Mantooth

Bb Instruments

TABLE OF CONTENTS

Page		CD Track
	tuning notes	1
4	Chapter I. Tonic Based Patterns	2
8	Chapter II. Rhythmic Displacement	3
12	Chapter III. Patterns Coupled	4
18	Chapter IV. Other Scale Degrees	5
20	Chapter V. Patterns Off Other Scale Steps	6
32	Chapter VI. Stringing the Patterns Together (part 1)	7
36	Chapter VII. Stringing the Patterns Together (part 2)	8
39	Chapter VIII. Minor Patterns	9
46	Chapter IX. Minor Workout	10

ISBN 0-7935-6855-2

7777 W. BLUEMOUND RD. P.O. BOX 13819 MILWAUKEE, WI 53213

Copyright © 1996 by HAL LEONARD CORPORATION
International Copyright Secured   All Rights Reserved

For all works contained herein:
Unauthorized copying, arranging, adapting, recording or public performance is an infringement of copyright.
Infringers are liable under the law.

Visit Hal Leonard on the internet at http://www.halleonard.com

FOREWORD

Many factors contributed to the release of this new method by Hal Leonard Corporation. There has been a recent proliferation of excellent improvisation texts and methods (e.g. those by David Baker, Jerry Coker, Jamey Aebersold, Mike Steinel, Shelton Berg, and Hal Crook, to mention only a few.) Despite this abundance of good materials, I am still amazed at how many students (and band directors) are still reliant on the printed sample solos provided by the arrangers of the various publishing houses. I have witnessed this "sample solo phenomenon" even at the college level.

Obviously, nothing is quite as educational as listening to the master improvisers. However, a recent statistic pointed out that the retail jazz market is a mere 1.2% of the record buying public. This statistic included the sales of compact discs and cassettes. Therefore, it is a safe assumption that not every child interested in "jazz band" wakes up listening to Bird or Trane at home. Radio airplay is monopolized today by rock, country, and talk radio. Even the classical market is substantially larger than the jazz.

YET, all ensembles under the jazz umbrella (stage bands, jazz ensembles, combos, salsa groups, fusion combos) are flourishing in today's curricula in the U.S. and Canada. High school and college festivals (both competitive and non-competitive) are boasting of record breaking entries and few cancellations. Considering this apparent renaissance of jazz, playing a sample solo reduces the jazz ensemble to a miniature concert band with a hi-hat. Too often in today's jazz ensemble rehearsals, the importance of improvisation is understated if not wholly ignored. Ironically, improvisation is the cornerstone of the art form.

Consequently, as an antidote to the sample solo dilemma, this method is designed to address the task (and hopefully, joy) of improvising. This method starts at square one and speaks to the kid (and band director) with absolutely no prior jazz experience. The patterns are simple. The accompanying rhythm tracks are (in this volume) all even or "straight" eighth grooves. This allows the student to learn accessible jazz vocabulary without being preoccupied at the same time with the triplet eighth swing concept.

Our aim is rapid progress in many different musical disciplines: sight-reading, aural awareness of chord progressions, theory, intervallic relationships, chord/scale relationships, and form as well as improvisation. To this objective we wish you an enjoyable adventure and much success.

Frank Mantooth

Acknowledgments

From The Beginning is the brainchild of many at Hal Leonard Corporation: John Cerullo, Tom Johns, Dan Rodowicz, Mike Sweeney, and Blair Bielawski. Special thanks to Tom Johns and Dan Rodowicz for their editorial assistance and invaluable experience in the fields of elementary school teaching, human psychology, and music editing.

FM

The Mission

From The Beginning has five primary objectives:

1. To eradicate any fears of improvisation.

2. To minimize tedious theoretical reading. The student will learn with the horn in his face (on the job training).

3. To teach form, harmonic awareness, theory, chord/scale relationships, and simple usable jazz vocabulary.

4. To instill a respect and appreciation for the art form and its practitioners.

5. To have fun.

Recording Information

Soundtrek Studio, Kansas City, Missouri
Ron Ubel, Engineer

Musicians:
Kim Park, Saxophones and Flute
Stan Kessler, Trumpet and Flugelhorn
Danny Embry, Guitar
Frank Mantooth, Piano
Bob Bowman, Bass
Todd Strait, Drums

tuning notes

I. TONIC BASED PATTERNS
(in order of complexity)

We'll begin with simple tonic based patterns. The advantage is that the first note the student plays is the same as the letter name of the chord symbol above that measure, e.g. if the chord symbol is C7, the the first note to play is "C". Think of these patterns as words or vocabulary. You'll be playing complete sentences in no time. Please pay attention to the printed articulations as well as the notes.

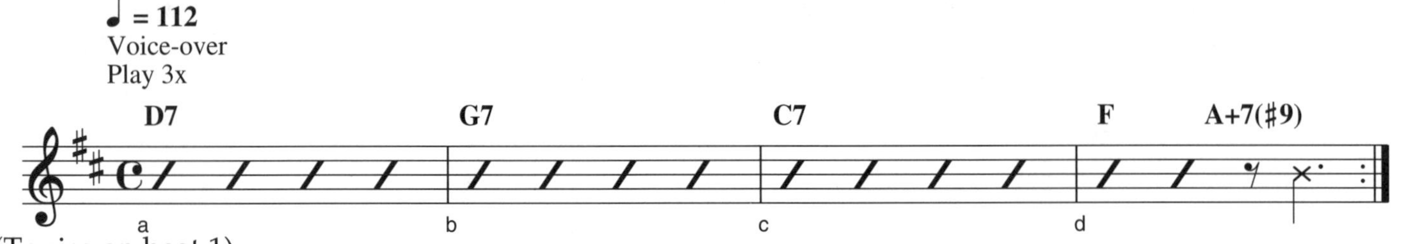

♩ = 112
Voice-over
Play 3x

I.1 (Tonics on beat 1)

I.2 (T-2-3)

Bb Instruments

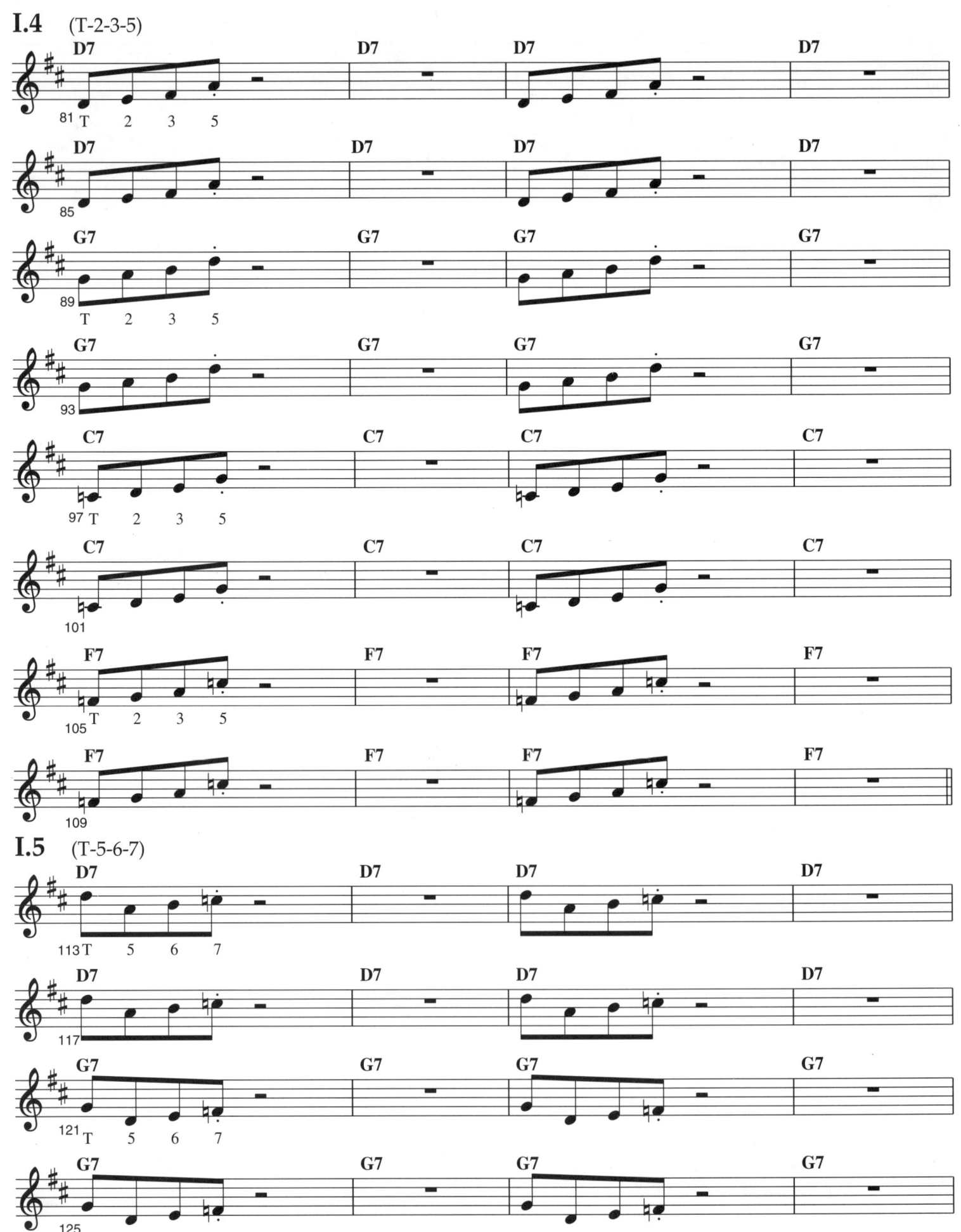

I.6 (T-Maj7-7-9-6-5)
(Courtesy of David Baker)

Bb Instruments

II. RHYTHMIC DISPLACEMENT
(after eighth and quarter rests)

Ellis Marsalis stresses the necessity of practicing phrases (lines, or patterns) starting at different places in the measure. To that end, the same patterns from Chapter I are printed after eighth and quarter rests. This practice puts the natural agogic accents on different notes in the pattern. The patterns will also become more deeply imbedded in the motor memory.

Bb Instruments

I.3 (T-2-#2-3)

II.4 (T-2-3-5)

Bb Instruments

III. PATTERNS COUPLED
(with rhythmic displacement)

It's now time for us to string together the different patterns. Random coupling of patterns (4 measures each) and rhythmic displacement will help us in our later attempts to make coherent musical sentences out of the vocabulary we've mastered.

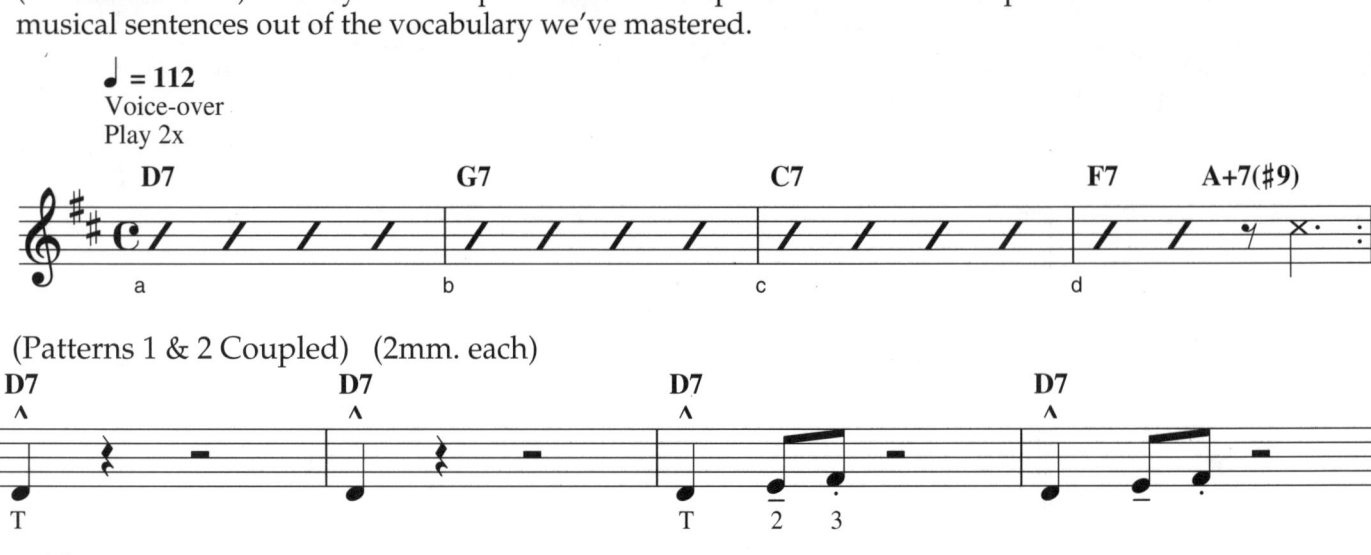

III.1 (Patterns 1 & 2 Coupled) (2mm. each)

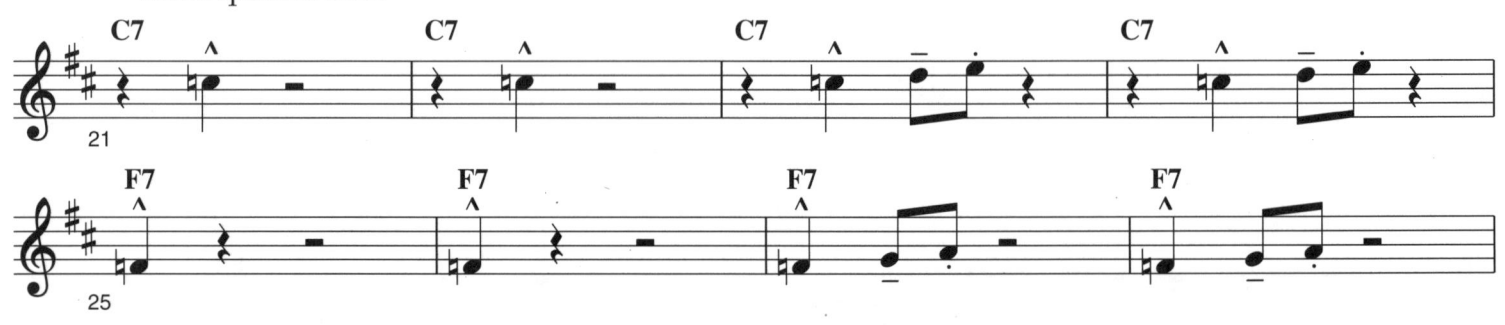

Bb Instruments

* Student may opt to tacet during even numbered measures to figure out upcoming pattern and rest the chops.
B♭ Instruments

14

III.4 (Patterns 1 & 6 Coupled)

Bb Instruments

III.5 (Patterns 1, 2 & 4 Coupled)

III.6 (Patterns 3 & 5 Coupled)

Bb Instruments

III.7 (Patterns 4 & 6 Coupled)

Bb Instruments

III.8 (Open Chorus - Free Swim)

B♭ Instruments

IV. OTHER SCALE DEGREES 5
(with rhythmic displacement)

Other possible diatonic starting tones are now introduced: the 2nd (9th), 3rd, 5th, 6th, and 7th. Play the desired note by using intellect alone.

♩ = 112
Voice-over
Play 2x

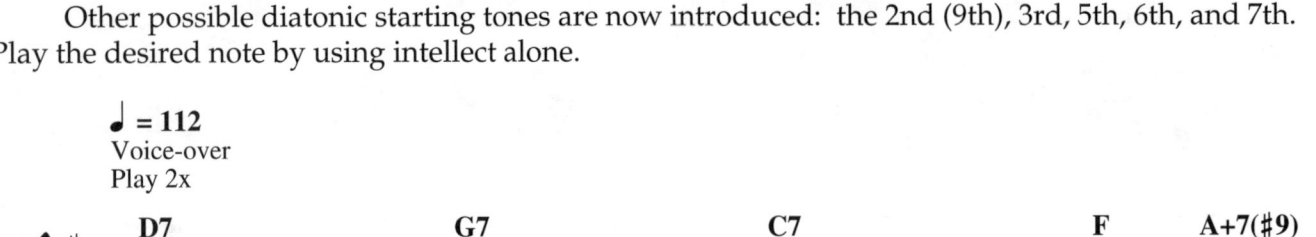

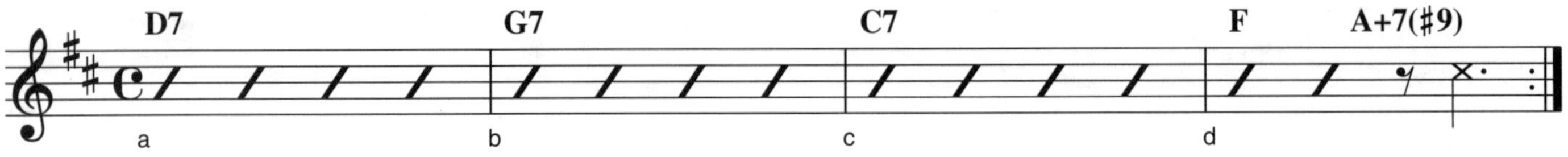

IV.1 (Play 2nds (9ths))

IV.2 (Play 3rds)

IV.3 (Play 5ths)

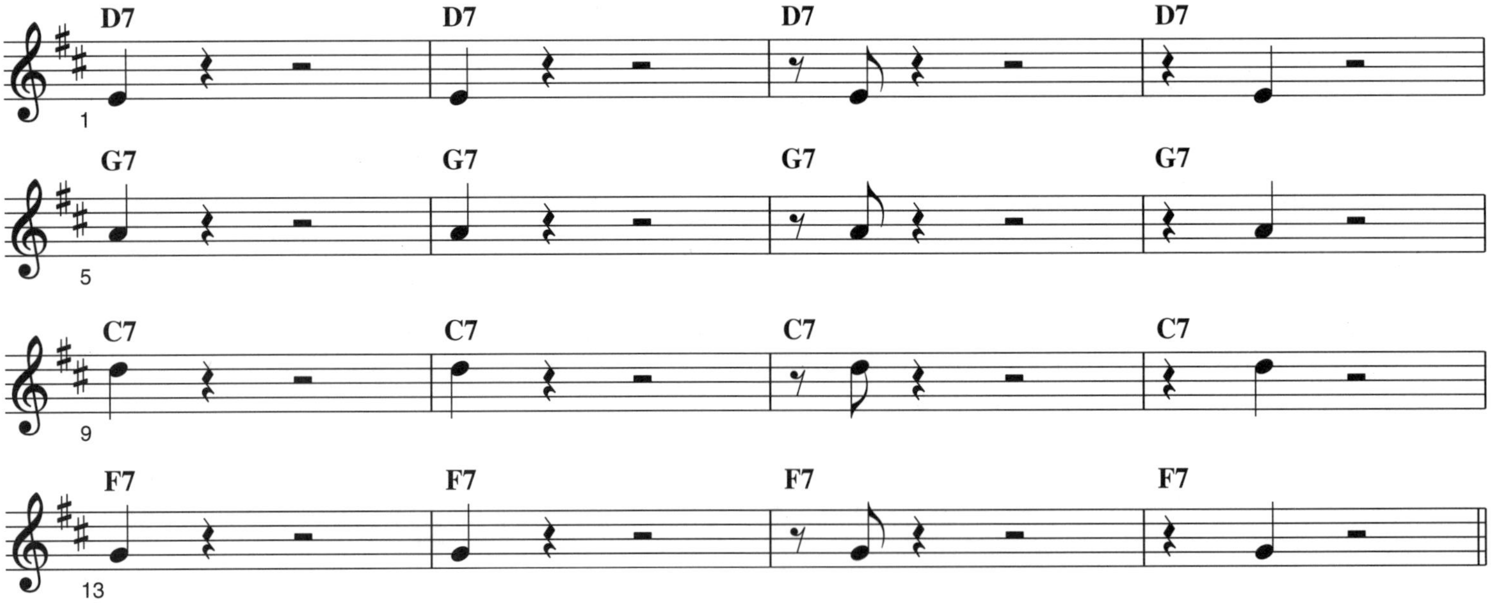

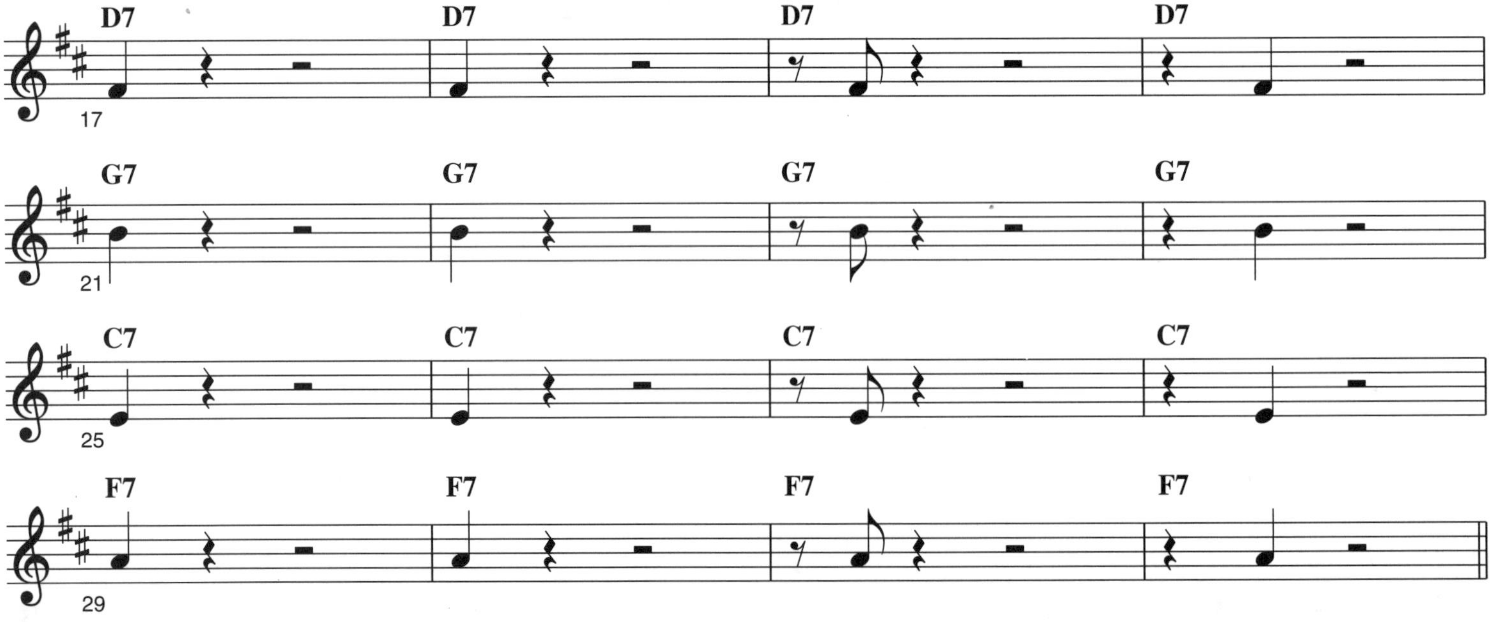

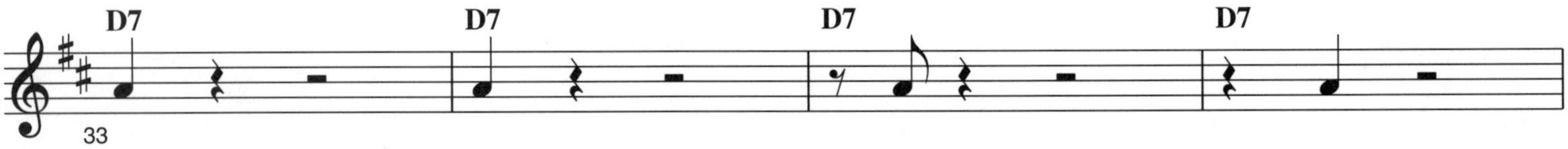

V. PATTERNS OFF OTHER SCALE STEPS
(with rhythmic displacement)

Let's now play patterns beginning from other starting tones. New patterns are introduced with rhythmic displacement to facilitate their memorization.

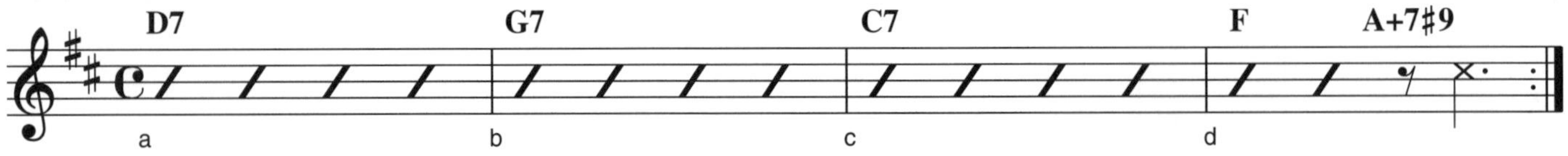

V.1 (From the 2nd (9th))

After eighth rest:

After quarter rest:

Bb Instruments

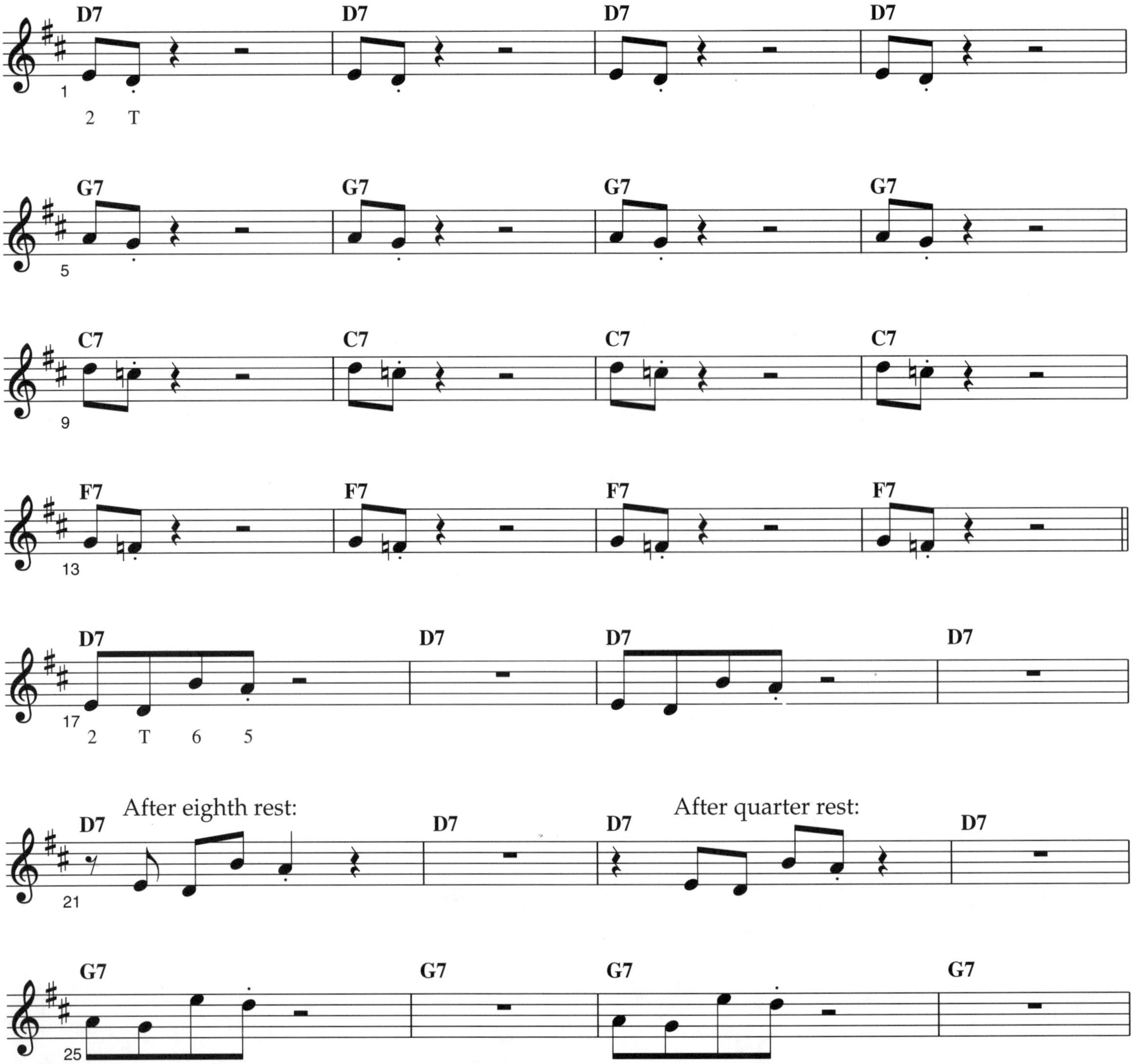

Bb Instruments

V.2 (From the 3rd)

Bb Instruments

Bb Instruments

Bb Instruments

V.8 (Open Chorus - Free Swim)

B♭ Instruments

VI. STRINGING THE PATTERNS TOGETHER (PART I)
(4 mm. per harmony)

Using the previously learned patterns, four sample solos over harmonies that last four measures each have been written out. Two new key centers are introduced: G and A♭. Patterns we've learned beginning on beat one appear on beat 4+ of the previous measure and are tied to beat one of the pattern. This practice is known as an anticipation or "shove". Two choruses are provided after the four sample choruses. These two "open choruses" are for you to play whatever comes to mind. Play the patterns you've learned or anything else you care to. The sky is the limit.

B♭ Instruments

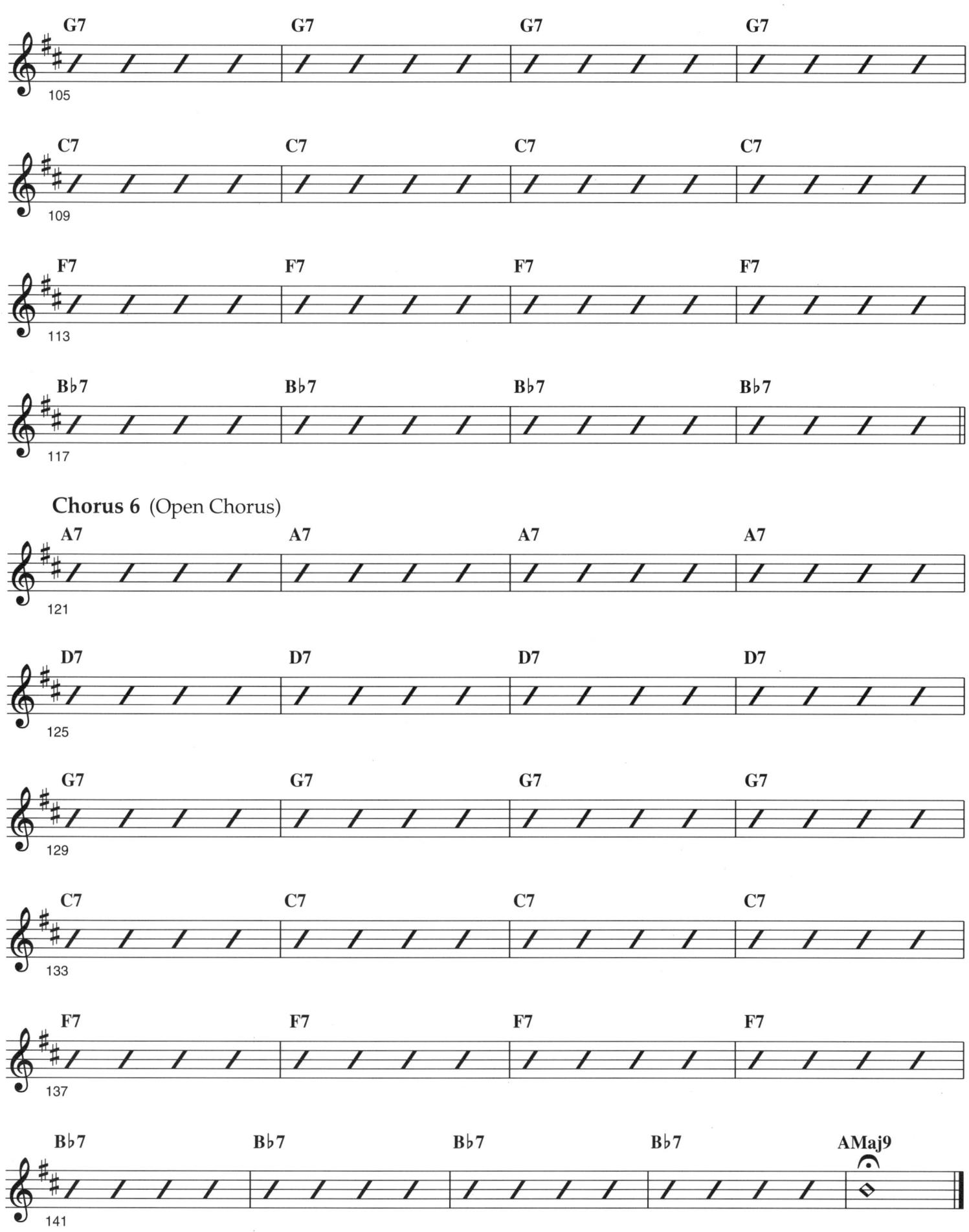

Bb Instruments

VII. STRINGING THE PATTERNS TOGETHER (PART 2)
(2 mm. per harmony)

This chapter uses the same vocabulary with rhythmic displacement and anticipations as the last chapter, but with shorter durations of each harmony. We'll see and hear a change of tonal center every two measures. Six sample choruses are offered. Four open choruses are provided for you to blow off some carbon (play what you like).

Bb Instruments

F7 F7 B♭7 B♭7
Chorus 4
A7 A7 D7 D7
G7 G7 C7 C7
F7 F7 B♭7 B♭7
Chorus 5
A7 A7 D7 D7
G7 G7 C7 C7
F7 F7 B♭7 B♭7
Chorus 6
A7 A7 D7 D7
G7 G7 C7 C7
F7 F7 B♭7 B♭7

Chorus 7 (Open Chorus)

A7	A7	D7	D7
G7	G7	C7	C7
F7	F7	B♭7	B♭7

Chorus 8 (Open Chorus)

A7	A7	D7	D7
G7	G7	C7	C7
F7	F7	B♭7	B♭7

Chorus 9 (Open Chorus)

A7	A7	D7	D7
G7	G7	C7	C7
F7	F7	B♭7	B♭7

Chorus 10 (Open Chorus)

A7	A7	D7	D7
G7	G7	C7	C7
F7	F7	B♭7	B♭7	AMaj9

B♭ Instruments

VIII. MINOR PATTERNS
(with rhythmic displacement)

Minor tonality patterns are now introduced. The previously learned major patterns can also be adapted by lowering the thirds one half step. The new minor patterns will be based off the following diatonic steps: Tonic, 2nd (9th), 3rd, 5th, 6th, and 7th.

VIII.1 (From the Tonic)

Bb Instruments

40

VIII.2 (From the 3rd)

B♭ Instruments

Bb Instruments

42

VIII.3 (From the 5th)

Bb Instruments

VIII.4 (From the 6th)

Bb Instruments

VIII.5 (From the 9th)

B♭ Instruments

B♭ Instruments

IX. A MINOR WORKOUT

(4 mm. per harmony)

Two sample solos of combined minor patterns are provided. Each harmony will have a four measure duration. There are three open choruses for self expression. Enjoy.

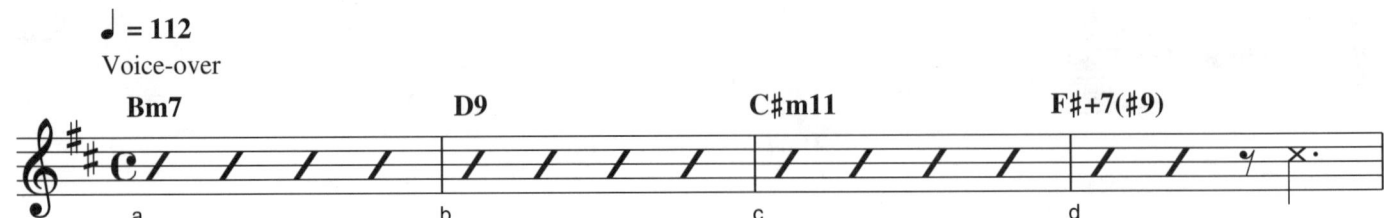

Bb Instruments

Chorus 3 (Open Chorus)

Chorus 4 (Open Chorus)

Bb Instruments

48

| Dm7 / / / | Dm7 / / / | Dm7 / / / | Dm7 / / / |

61

Chorus 5   (Open Chorus)

| Bm7 / / / | Bm7 / / / | Bm7 / / / | Bm7 / / / |

65

| Em7 / / / | Em7 / / / | Em / / / | Em7 / / / |

69

| Am7 / / / | Am7 / / / | Am7 / / / | Am7 / / / |

73

| Dm7 / / / | Dm7 / / / | Dm7 / / / | Dm7 / / / |

77

Chorus 6   (Open Chorus)

| Bm7 / / / | Gm7 / / / | Bm7 / / / | Bm7 / / / |

81

| Em7 / / / | Em7 / / / | Em7 / / / | Em7 / / / |

85

| Am7 / / / | Am7 / / / | Am7 / / / | Am7 / / / |

89

| Dm7 / / / | Dm7 / / / | Dm7 / / / | Dm7 / / / | Bm11 𝄐 |

93

B♭ Instruments

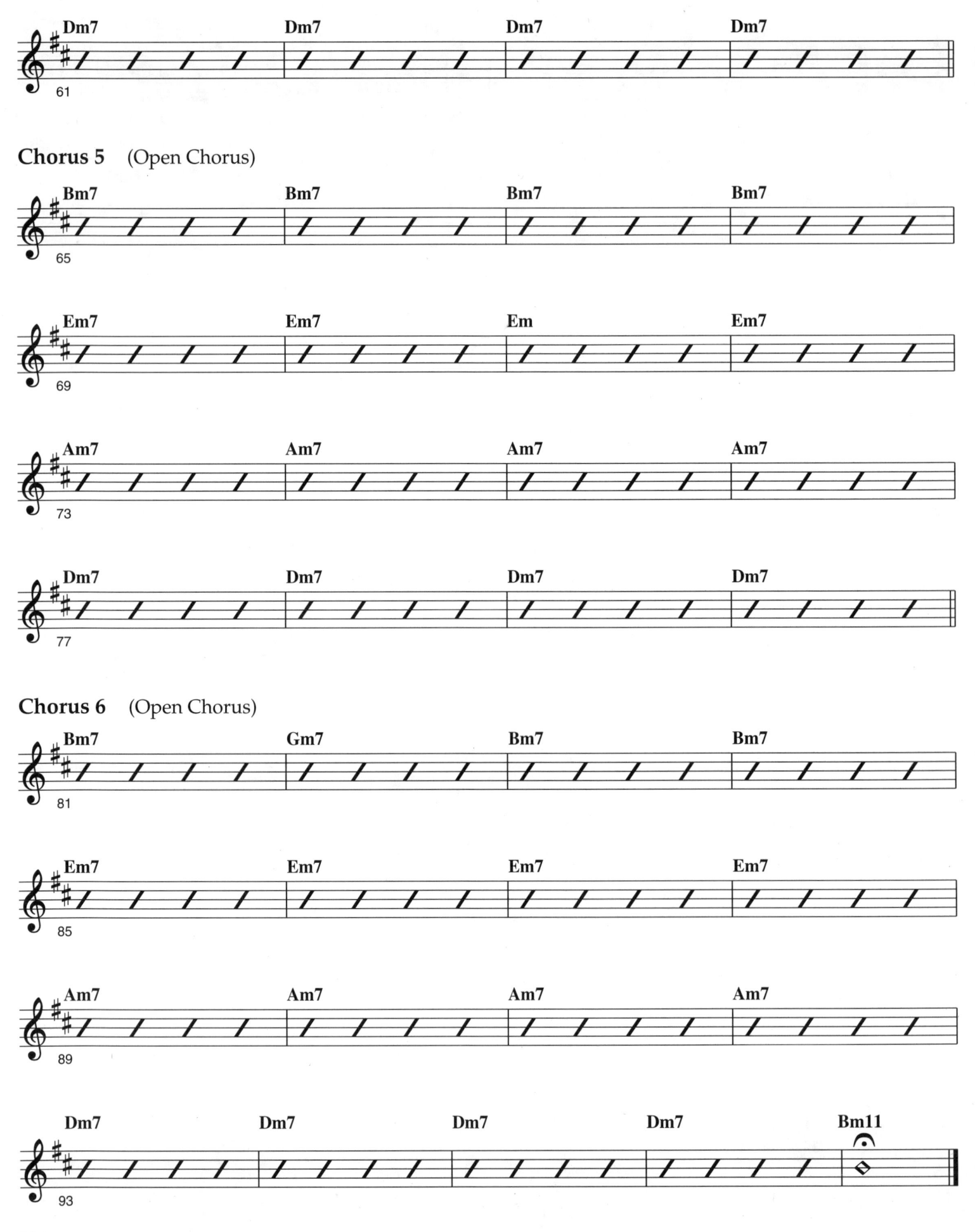